BEBOP GUITAR
SOLOS

MICHAEL KAPLAN

Edited by Jonathan Feist

Berklee Press

Editor in Chief: Jonathan Feist
Vice President of Online Learning and Continuing Education: Debbie Cavalier
Assistant Vice President of Operations for Berklee Media: Robert F. Green
Assistant Vice President of Marketing and Recruitment for Berklee Media: Mike King
Dean of Continuing Education: Carin Nuernberg
Editorial Assistants: Matthew Dunkle, Reilly Garrett, Zoë Lustri, José Rodrigo Vazquez
Cover Design: Small Mammoth Design

ISBN 978-0-87639-143-3

1140 Boylston Street
Boston, MA 02215-3693 USA
(617) 747-2146

Visit Berklee Press Online at
www.berkleepress.com

Study with

■ **BERKLEE ONLINE**

online.berklee.edu

DISTRIBUTED BY

HAL•LEONARD®
CORPORATION
7777 W. BLUEMOUND RD. P.O. BOX 13819
MILWAUKEE, WISCONSIN 53213

Visit Hal Leonard Online at
www.halleonard.com

Berklee Press, a publishing activity of Berklee College of Music, is a not-for-profit educational publisher.
Available proceeds from the sales of our products are contributed to the scholarship funds of the college.

CONTENTS

INTRODUCTION

These solos were transcribed from some of the most influential jazz guitarists, and a tremendous amount of information can be learned from them. Their original recording is noted in the section about each tune, and it is imperative to listen to the recordings of the transcriptions, preferably before playing them. I strongly suggest being able to first sing or, at minimum, hear the solo in your head, before playing them. By doing so, a quicker assimilation from the notes on the pages to the guitar can be accomplished.

The tablature for each solo is a suggestion, instead of a "must be played this way." There are many different ways to play the same phrase on the instrument, and ultimately, that decision is for you to make. Regardless of what position and fingering you decide to use, it is my belief that you need to "see" the chord and scale underlying each phrase. That being said, I propose that you start with the string choices shown in the tablature. If it does not suit you, search for an alternative. After all, this is jazz, and everyone comes at it from his or her own perspective. All of the musicians who created these solos are jazz guitarists, but they all play differently and approach fingering from their own perspective.

There is no recommended order to these transcriptions; start wherever you choose. If you listen to a solo, it moves you, and you feel inspired by it, then go ahead and begin with that one. If along the way you find that you like a specific guitarist's playing, I encourage you to seek out more recordings by that artist, and dig deeper into their specific style of improvisation. Many times, you will find that a musician has a certain method to their playing that is quite consistent and predictable. In addition, I suggest putting the phrases that you like in all keys.

There is much more to jazz than just theory. In fact, not until you go deep into the history, culture, and classic recordings of jazz can you fully grasp it. So dive in and study these solos from some of the best jazz guitarists that ever were! Sadly, George Benson is the only guitarist still living, out of the artists selected for this book. However, there is a wealth of information contained in the playing of the guitarists that came before us, and we can learn a lot from them. I know I did, and continue to.

—*Michael Kaplan*

"I'll Remember April"

"I'll Remember April" is from the Grant Green album *Standards*. It features Wilbur Ware on bass and Al Harewood on drums. The album was recorded on August 29, 1961 for Blue Note and was released in 1998, although six of the eight tunes were previously released in Japan in 1980, on the record *Remembering* .

One of the main ideas that you can take away from this solo and incorporate into your playing immediately is Grant's way of playing a minor triad over a major chord. Some permutation of this singular concept is used more than a dozen times in this solo. It happens three times in the first fifteen bars alone.

Here are some examples using an E minor triad over G major:

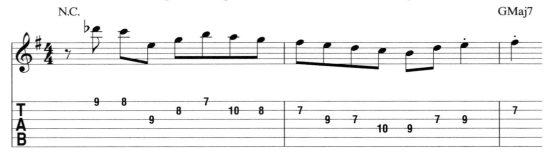

FIG. 1.1. "I'll Remember April" Measures 1–2

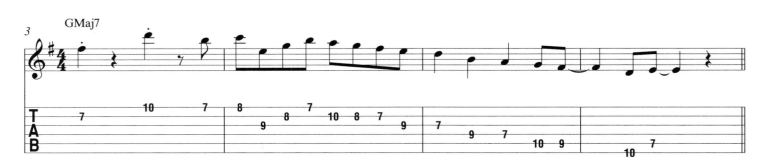

FIG. 1.2. "I'll Remember April" Measures 3–6

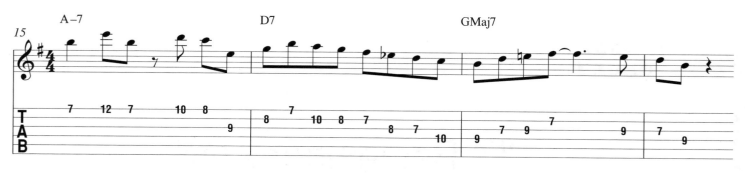

FIG. 1.3. "I'll Remember April" Measures 15–18

Notice how the E minor triad is used in every example. All of the preceding examples descend the same after the triad with the exception of figure 1.3. In this phrase, one note is changed. The E is replaced with an E♭ over the D7 chord creating a D7(♭9) chord. This creates tension and a stronger pull and resolution on the GMaj7 chord.

I'LL REMEMBER APRIL
Solo by Grant Green

Words and Music by Pat Johnston,
Don Raye and Gene De Paul

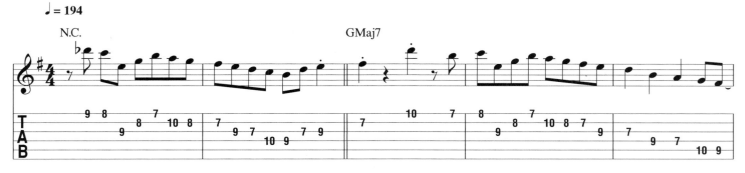

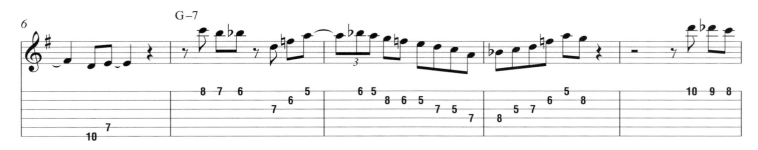

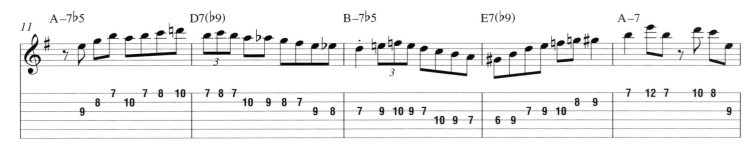

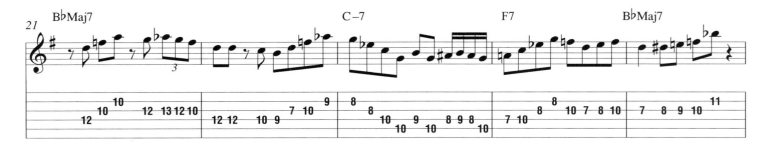

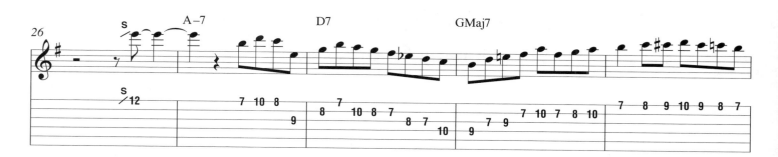

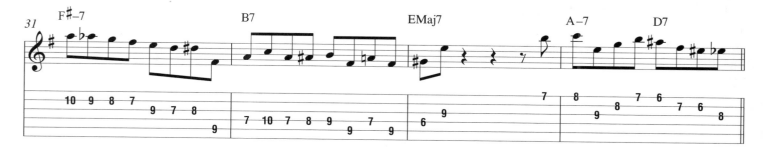

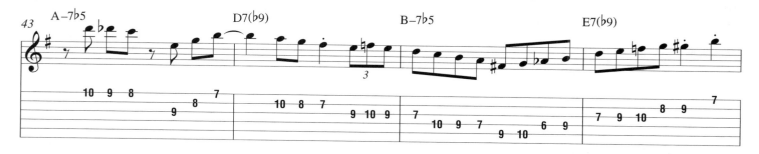

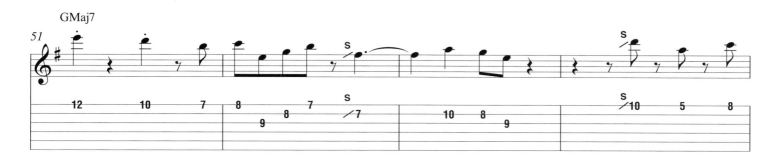

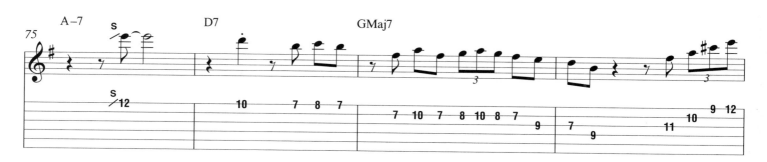

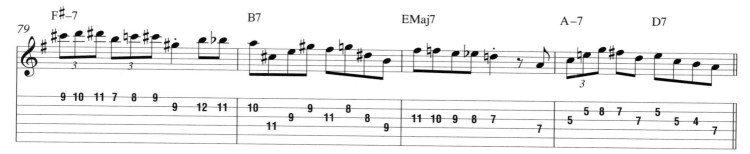

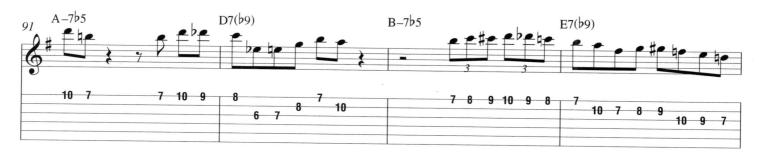

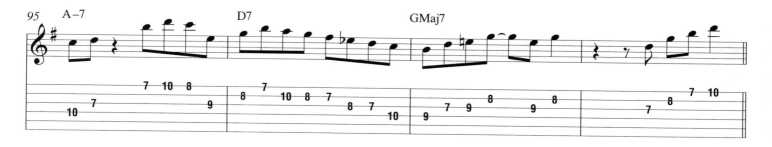

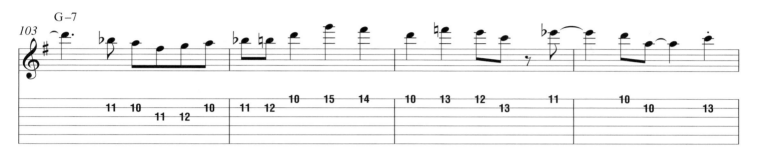

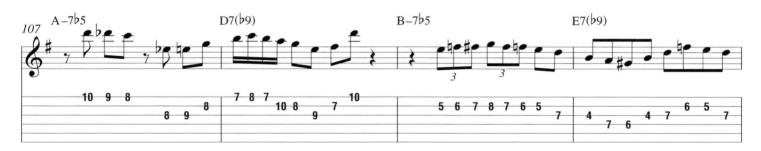

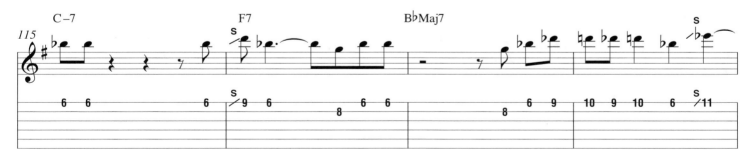

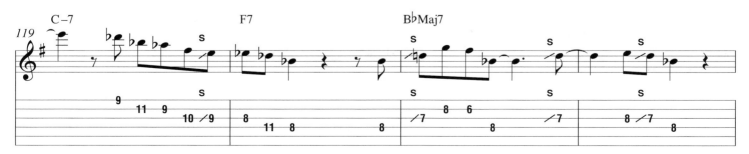

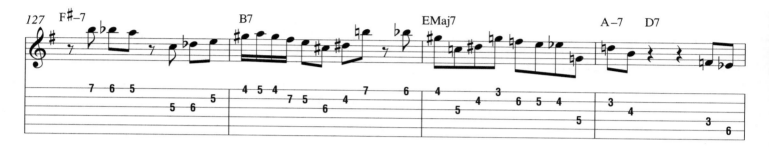

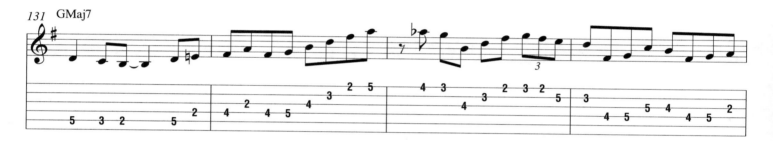

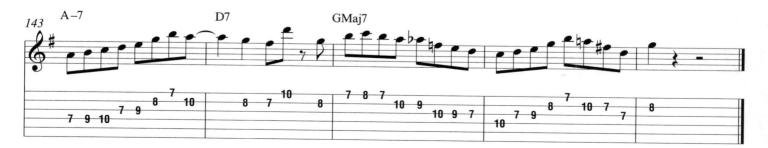

FIG. 1.4. "I'll Remember April" Complete Solo

"You and the Night and the Music"

"You and the Night and the Music" is also on Grant Green's *Standards* album. In this transcription, we will look at how he uses the 3, 5, 7, and ♭9 of a dominant chord, which is a very big part of the bebop vocabulary. In addition, note his use of sixteenth notes and triplets throughout the solo.

Figure 2.1 (measures 25–26) shows the use of the 3, 5, 7, and ♭9 (C♯, E, G, B♭) concept over an A7(♭9) chord. The phrase resolves on the 3 (F) of the D–7 chord.

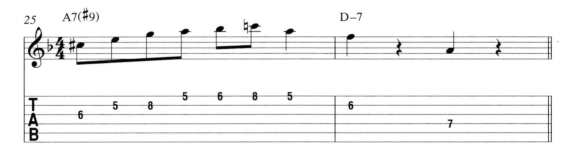

FIG. 2.1. "You and the Night and the Music" Excerpt, Measures 25–26

Figure 2.2 (measures 6–8 and 14–16) shows Grant's use of sixteenth notes along with the same concept being employed over the A7(♭9) chord. However, this time, he descends from the 3 (C♯) to the 5 (E) instead of ascending.

FIG. 2.2. "You and the Night and the Music" Measures 6–8

Figure 2.3 (measures 41–43) shows sixteenth notes and triplets, as well as both versions of the 3, 5, 7, and ♭9 concept.

FIG. 2.3. "You and the Night and the Music" Measures 41–43

YOU AND THE NIGHT AND THE MUSIC
Solo by Grant Green

Words by Howard Dietz
Music by Arthur Schwartz

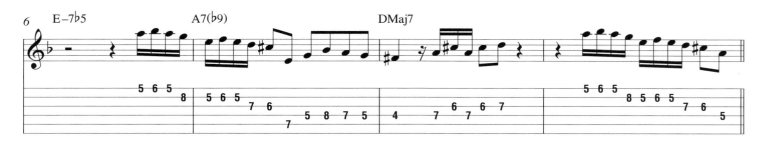

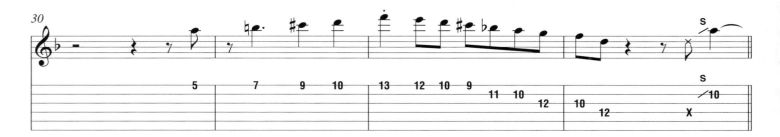

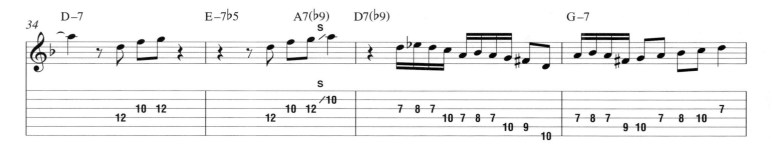

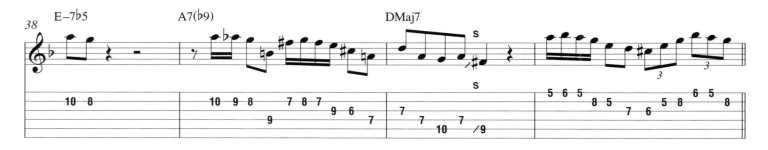

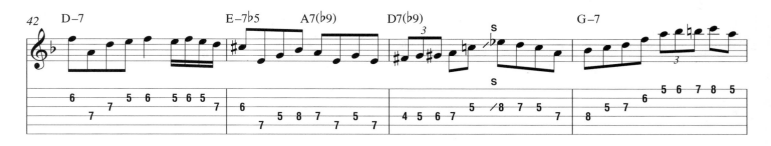

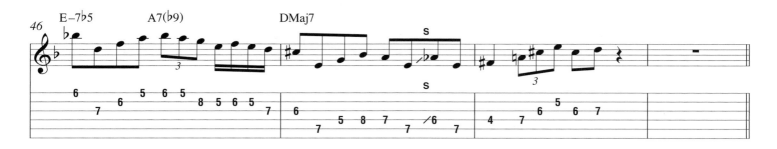

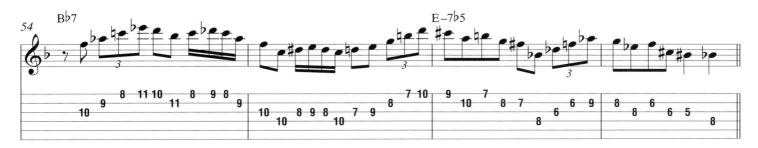

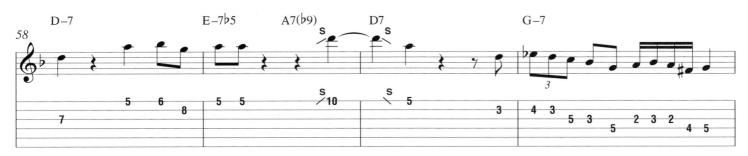

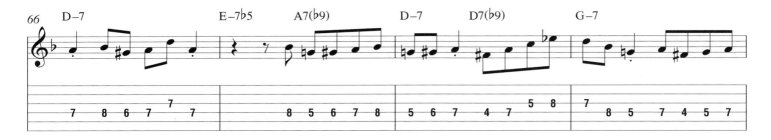

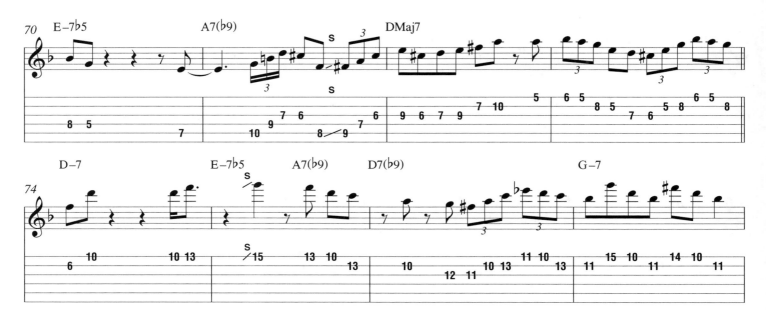

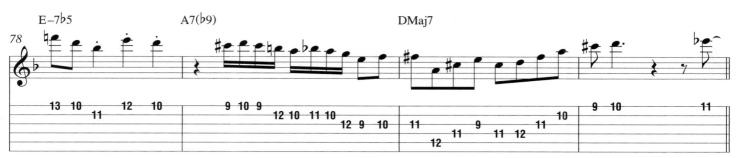

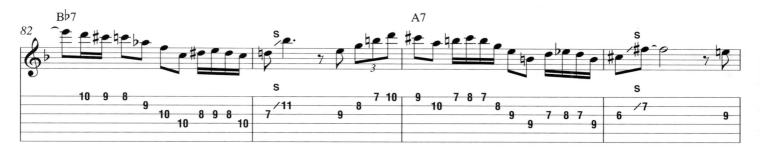

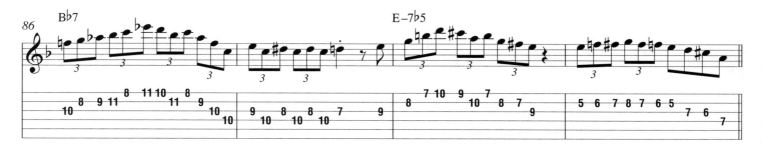

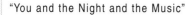

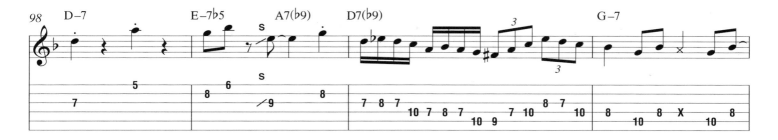

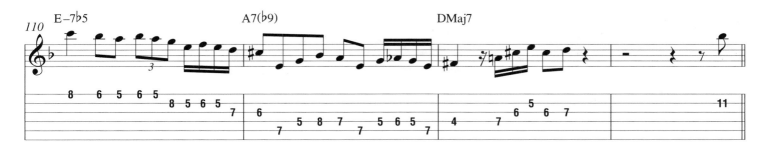

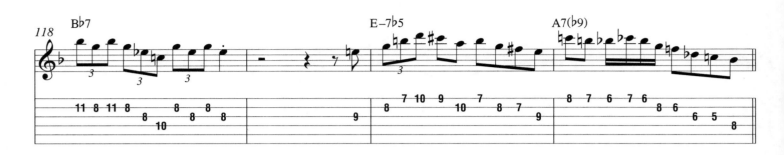

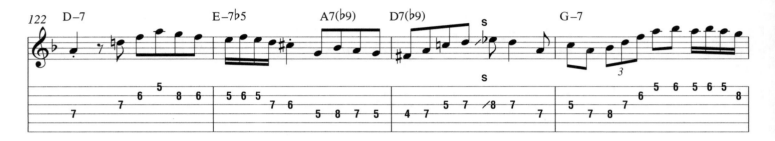

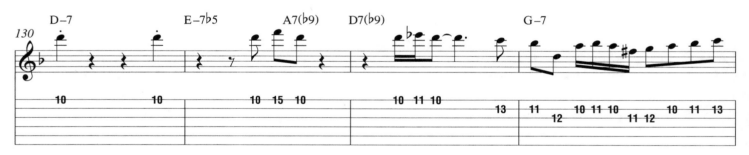

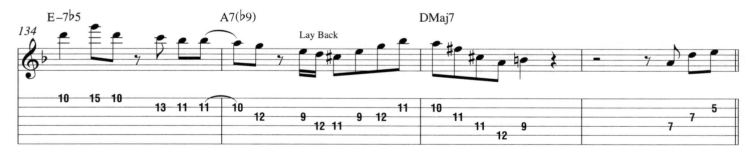

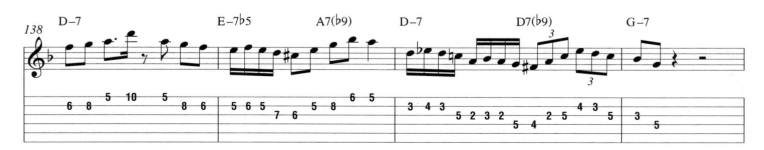

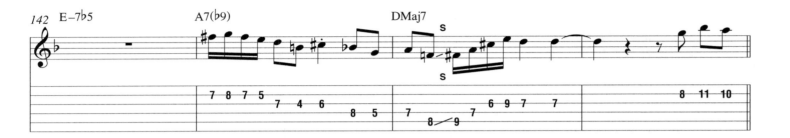

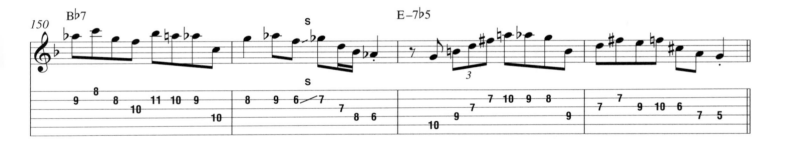

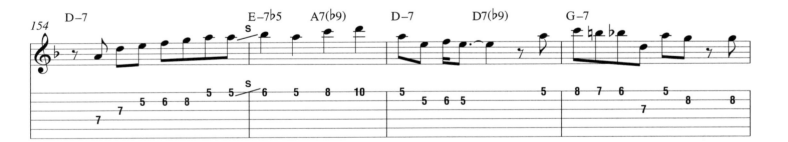

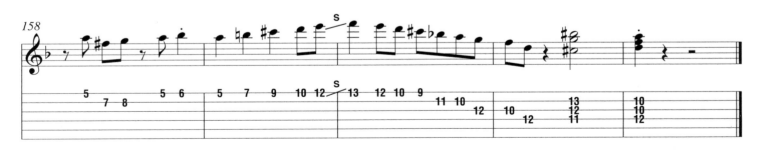

FIG. 2.4. "You and the Night and the Music" Complete Solo

3. JIMMY RANEY

"Have You Met Miss Jones?"

"Have You Met Miss Jones?" is from the album *Jimmy Raney Visits Paris*. It was recorded on February 10, 1954. The lineup included Bobby Jaspar on tenor sax, Roger Guerin on trumpet, Maurice Vander on piano, Jean-Marie Ingrand on bass, and Jean-Louis Viale on drums.

In the following three examples, we will look at another very important piece of bebop vocabulary.

Figure 3.1 (measures 12–14) shows Jimmy landing on the 3 of the G–7 chord (Bb) and then descending a minor sixth to the 5 (D) and playing a D minor triad, which produces the 5, 7, and 9 of the G–7 chord.

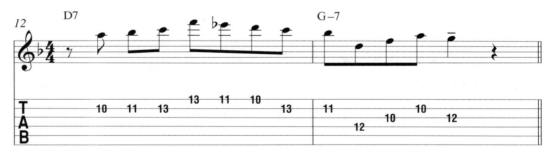

FIG. 3.1. "Have You Met Miss Jones?" Measures 12–14

Figure 3.2 (measures 17–19) shows the same concept, this time over a C–7 chord.

FIG. 3.2. "Have You Met Miss Jones?" Measures 17–19

Figure 3.3 (measures 49–51) is exactly the same as figure 3.1, but played over a different chord. Because of this, it makes him land on the 7 of the C minor (B♭) instead of the 3 as in of G minor as shown in figure 3.1.

FIG. 3.3. "Have You Met Miss Jones?" Measures 49–51

One other thing to notice is how figures 3.2 and 3.3 descend the same over the F7 chord using the ♭9 (G♭) and resolve with the same phrase starting on the 3 (D) of the B♭Maj7 chord.

HAVE YOU MET MISS JONES?
Solo by Jimmy Raney

Words by Lorenz Hart
Music by Richard Rodgers

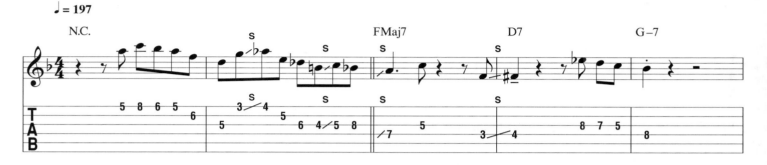

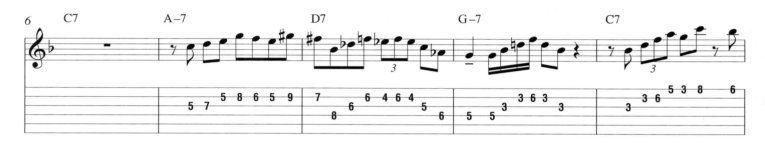

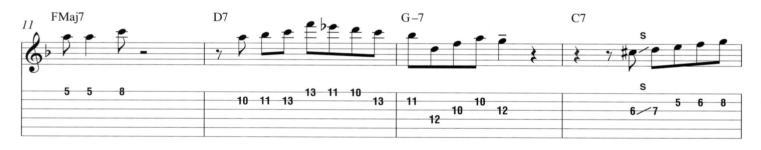

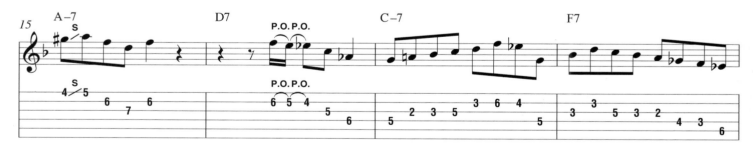

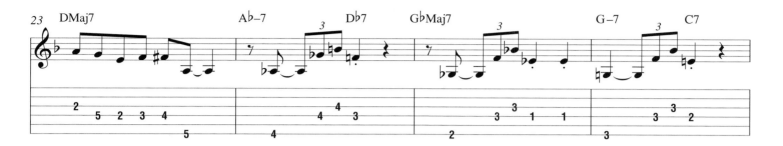

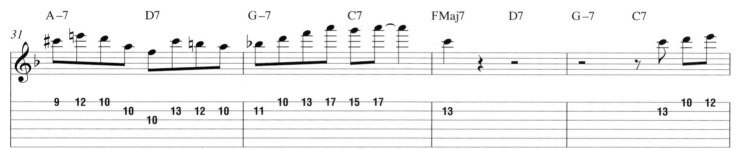

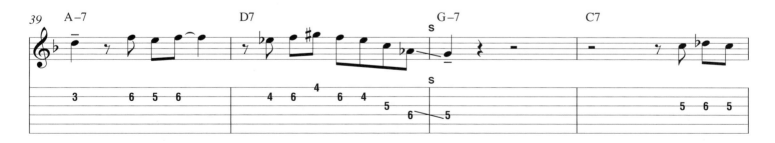

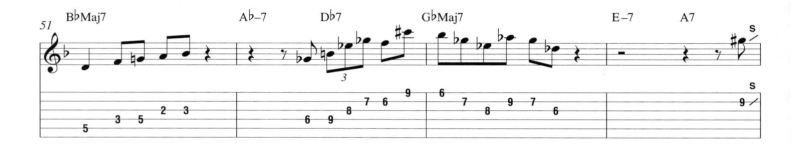

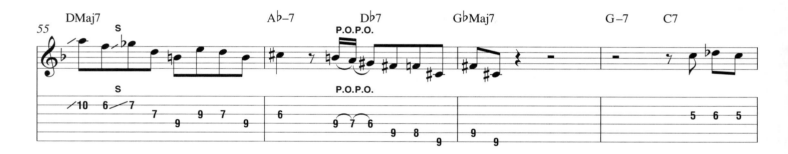

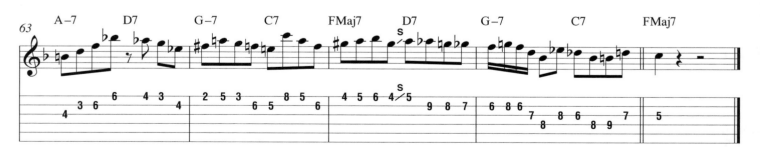

FIG. 3.4. "Have You Met Miss Jones?" Complete Solo

4. JIMMY RANEY

"Fascinating Rhythm"

"Fascinating Rhythm" is from the same album as "Have You Met Miss Jones?" We are going to look at two different concepts from this transcription in addition to the same concept from the "Have You Met Miss Jones?" transcription.

Figure 4.1 (measures 3–4) and 2 (measures 35–37) are the widely used major 7 over a minor 7 chord.

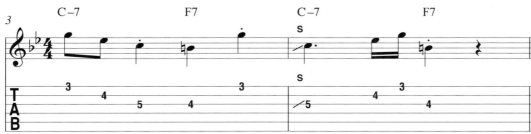

FIG. 4.1. "Fascinating Rhythm" Measures 3–4

FIG. 4.2. "Fascinating Rhythm" Measures 35–37

In figure 4.3 (Intro lick) and figure 4.4 (measures 11–13), he alters the V chord of a II V I progression by playing the ♯9 and ♭9.

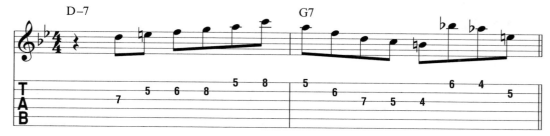

FIG. 4.3. "Fascinating Rhythm" Measures 1–2

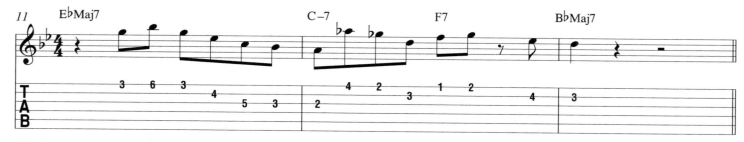

FIG. 4.4. "Fascinating Rhythm" Measures 11–13

Figures 4.5 to 4.7 utilize a concept that we discussed in "Have You Met Miss Jones?"

FIG. 4.5. "Fascinating Rhythm" Measures 31–33

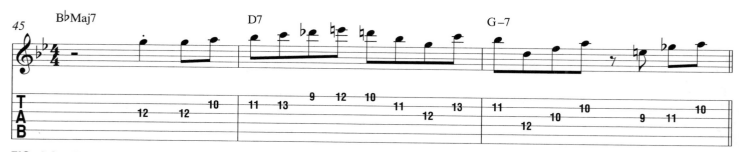

FIG. 4.6. "Fascinating Rhythm" Measures 45–47

FIG. 4.7. "Fascinating Rhythm" Measures 60–62

FASCINATING RHYTHM
Solo by Jimmy Raney

Music and Lyrics by George Gershwin
and Ira Gershwin

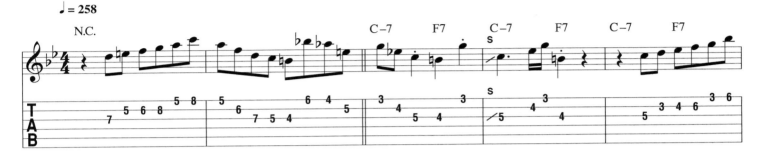

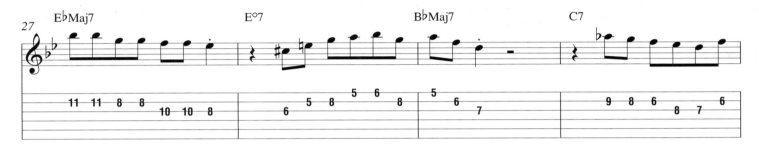

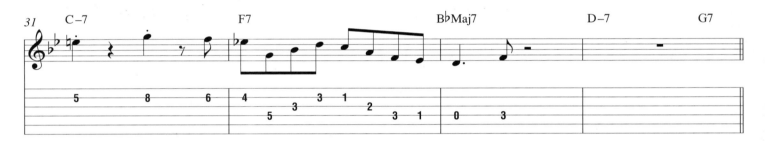

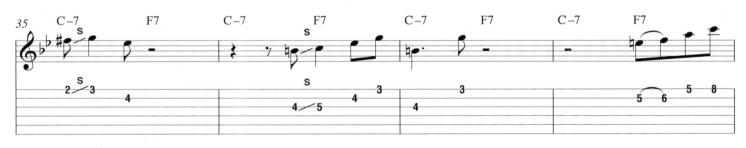

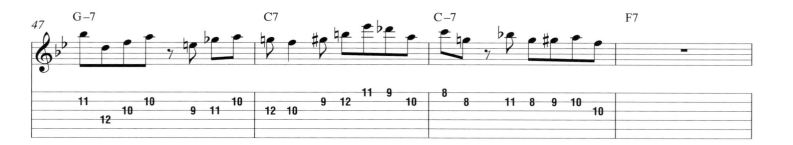

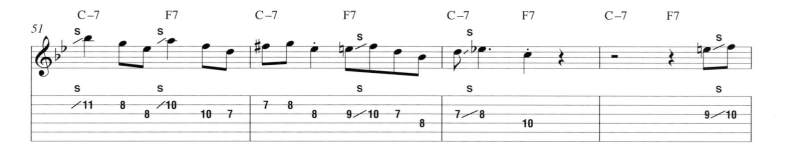

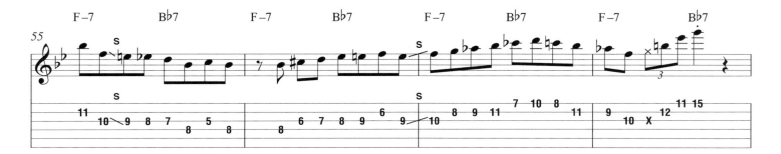

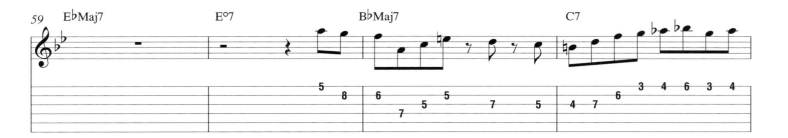

FIG. 4.8. "Fascinating Rhythm" Complete Solo

5. JOE PASS

"Oleo"

"Oleo" was recorded on Joe Pass' duo album *Chops*, with renowned Danish bassist Niels-Henning Ørsted Pedersen. It was recorded on November 19, 1978 and released the same year. It was reissued in 1993 on CD by Original Jazz Classics. Let's look at how Joe plays the bridge of all dominant 7 chords descending in fourths.

Figure 5.1 (measures 17–24) starts with a descending D major triad. Next, the 13, 7, 5, and 11 are played before landing on the major 7 of the G7 chord where he encloses (plays a note above and below) the ♭7. Joe then plays an A minor triad (9, 11, and 13 of G7), followed by the 5 and the 11 of the G7, from which he plays from the 9 chromatically to the 3 where he plays the 3, 5, 7, 9. The first measure of the C7 chord (measure 21) is basically scalar with the exception of the ♭9 and major 7, which enclose the root (C) of the C7 chord (on the downbeat of measure 22). Also, in the second measure of the C7 chord, he starts by playing down a whole step and up a half step. This is a popular bebop phrase that could be extended indefinitely. Over the F7 chord, he starts by playing chromatically before eventually playing the alterations of #5, ♭9, and #11.

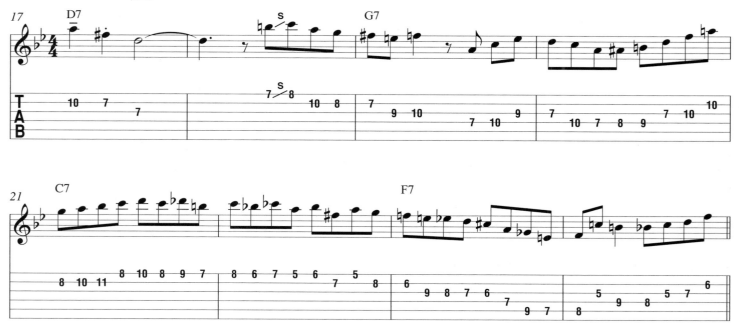

FIG. 5.1. "Oleo" Measures 17–24

Figure 5.2 (measures 49–56) begins with a very cool eighth-note triplet phrase over the D7 chord. First, he plays the 3 and the ♯9 as two eighth notes. This is followed by four eighth-note triplet patterns where he plays the root, ♭9, root, then the 13, 7, and 13, again the root, ♭9, root, ♯9, 3, ♯9, and finally the major 7, 9, and root. Over the G7 chord he plays the ♯9, 3, root, ♭9, root, and 7 in the first measure proceeded by the 13, 3, ♯9, ♭9, root and 7, before going to the 5 and ascending chromatically into the 3 of C7.

Measure 53 starts on the 3 (E) of the C7 chord and ascends up the scale to the 7 (B♭) where he proceeds to play a B♭ major 9 arpeggio starting from beat 2 of the measure. From there he plays straight down the C bebop scale. Over the F7 chord, he plays an A–7♭5 arpeggio (also the 3, 5, 7, and 9 of F7).

FIG. 5.2. "Oleo" Measures 49–56

In figure 5.3 (measures 81–88), Joe plays the 3, ♭9, and root of D7. He then descends straight down the D Mixolydian scale starting from the 9. This goes into the 3 of the G7 where you again have a popular phrase of the 3, 5, 11 and ♯9 going into the 3, 5, 7, and 9. Over the C7 he plays chromatically descending from the root, hits the 9, goes down the scale putting in the ♯9 and then plays the 3, root, and chromatic to the 7 where he proceeds to play the root, 9, and 11. It is important to see that this could be seen as the Coltrane pattern of 1, 2, 3, 5 but of the B♭ major chord. Finally, over the F7 he plays a bunch of chromatic eighth-note triplet figures, which are identical but move up in minor thirds (another important concept to be aware of).

FIG. 5.3. "Oleo" Measures 81–88

OLEO
Solo by Joe Pass

By Sonny Rollins

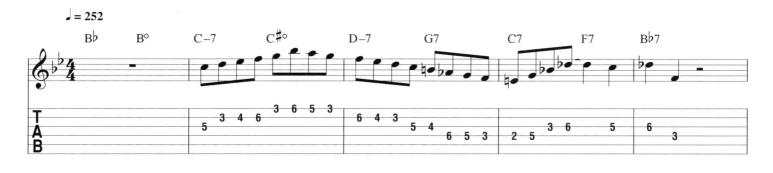

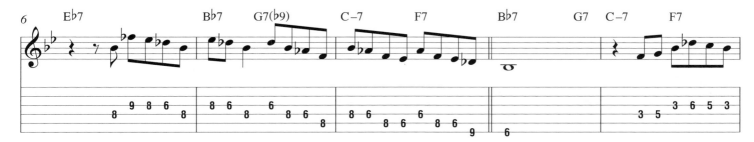

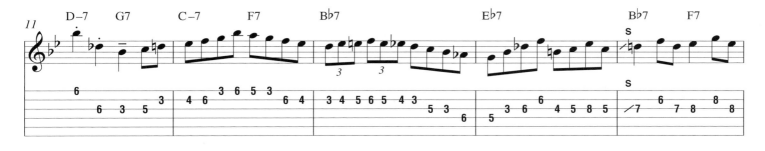

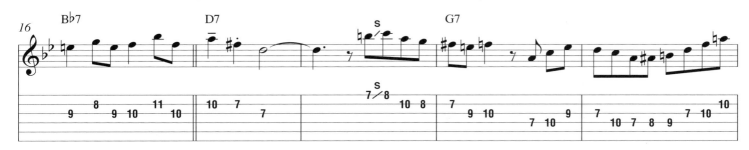

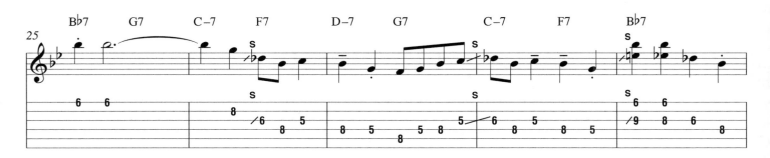

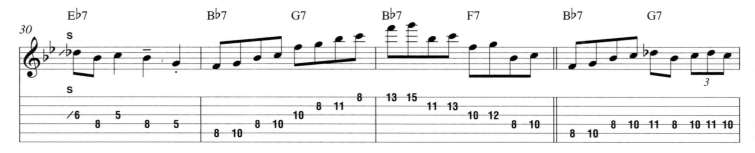

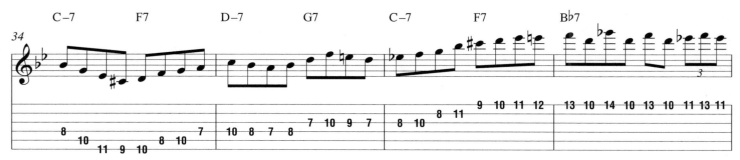

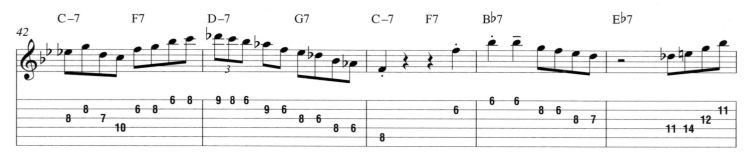

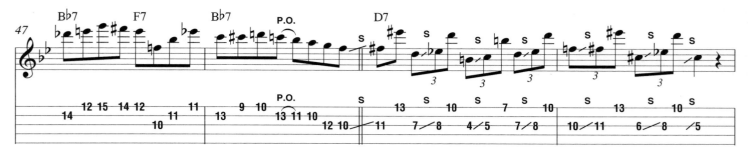

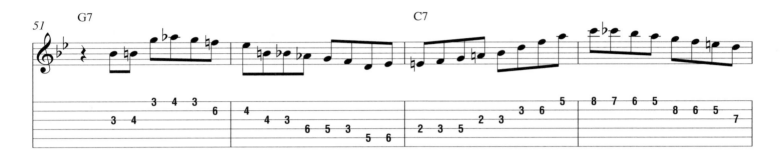

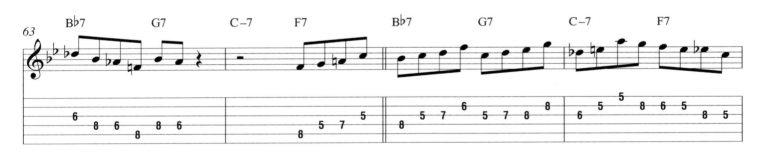

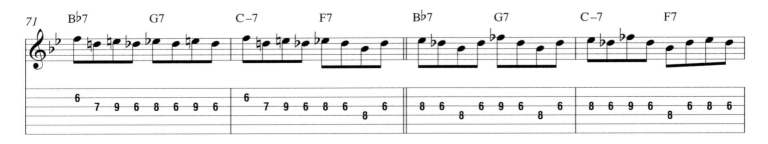

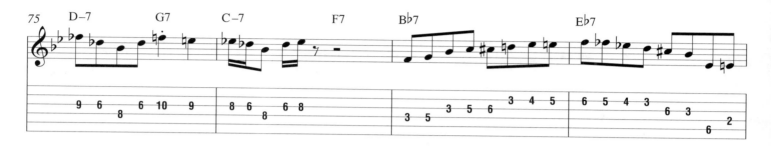

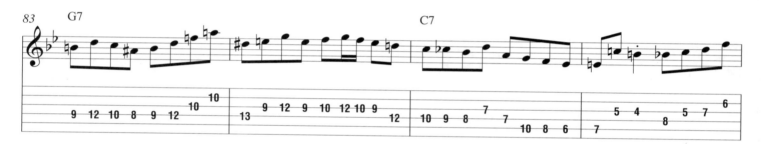

FIG. 5.4. "Oleo" Complete Solo

6. JOE PASS

"Tricotism"

"Tricotism" was recorded on the *Chops* album as well. Being that the blues is a large part of bebop vocabulary, we will look at four examples of how Joe utilizes blues phrases.

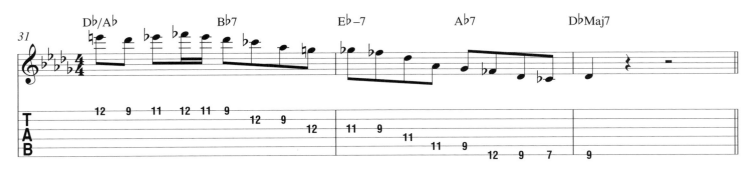

FIG. 6.1. "Tricotism" Measures 31–33

FIG. 6.2. "Tricotism" Measures 42–43

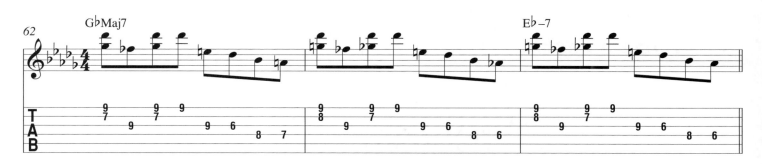

FIG. 6.3. "Tricotism" Measures 62–64

In figure 6.4 (measures 96–98), notice his use of fourths in the second measure.

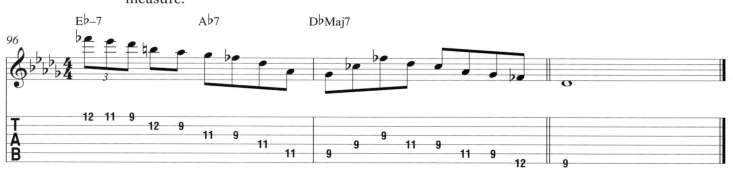

FIG. 6.4. "Tricotism" Measures 96–98

TRICOTISM
Solo by Joe Pass

By Oscar Pettiford

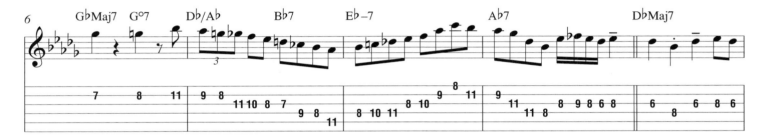

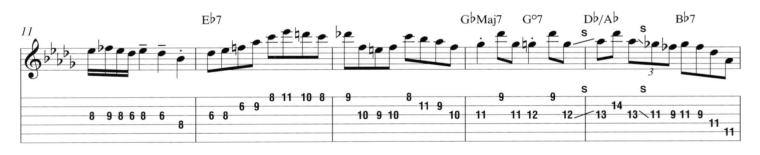

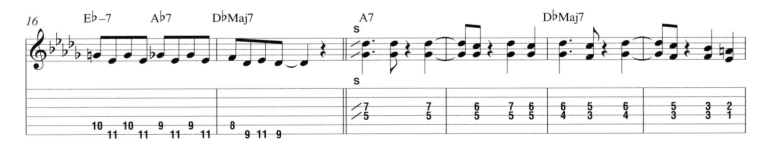

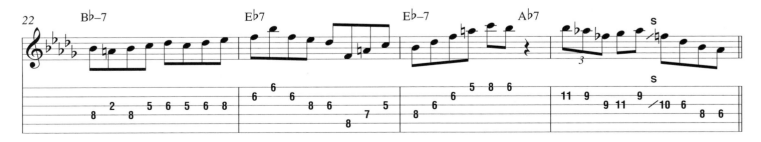

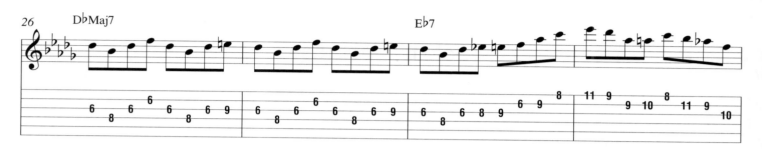

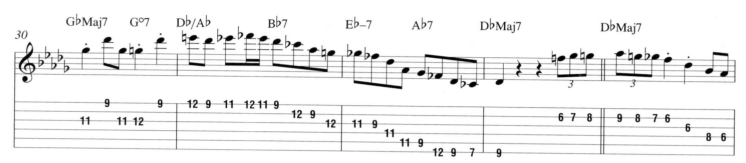

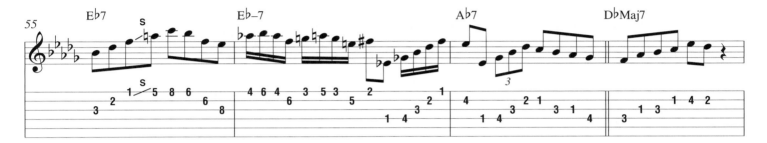

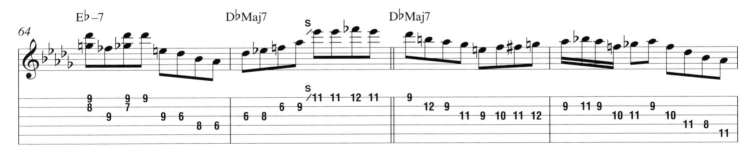

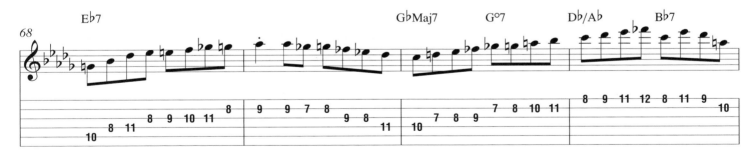

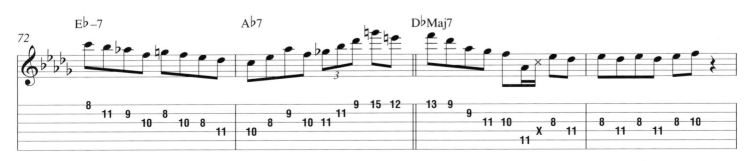

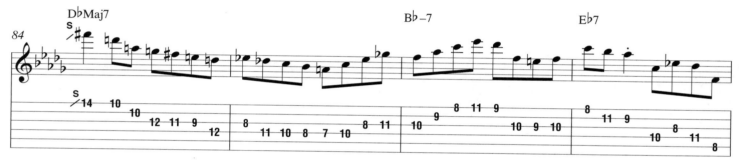

FIG. 6.5. "Tricotism" Complete Solo

"Four on Six"

This version of "Four on Six" comes from Wes's fourth album, aptly named *The Incredible Jazz Guitar of Wes Montgomery*. The personnel include Tommy Flanagan on piano, Percy Heath on bass, and Albert Heath on drums. The album is regarded by many to be the peak of Wes's work.

In this transcription, we will look at five different examples as to how Wes negotiates his way through the bridge of the tune, which consists of four different II V chord progressions lasting for only one measure apiece.

In figure 7.1 (measures 6–9), he plays the 3 of the C–7 chord followed by the root, 13, and 5 of the F7 chord. In the next measure, he plays the root, 5, and 7 of the B♭–7 chord followed by the 5 and root of the E♭7 chord. Next is a quick sixteenth-note chromatic pull-off descending from the 5 of the A–7 to the root of the D7 chord. Lastly, he sequences the same rhythmic idea over the E♭–7 chord from the 9 chromatically down to the root, and from there descends straight down the E♭ Dorian or A♭ Mixolydian scale.

FIG. 7.1. "Four on Six" Measures 6–9

Figure 7.2 (measures 22–25) has Wes playing an E♭ major triad (Wes loved to think major over minor) or the 3, 5, and 7 of C minor followed by the 3 and root of the F7 chord. The next three measures show Wes thinking of only the II chord. Note how smoothly he gets from the E♭7 chord into the A minor chord.

FIG. 7.2. "Four on Six" Measures 22–25

Figure 7.3 (measures 38–41) shows Wes thinking again of only the II chord of each chord progression.

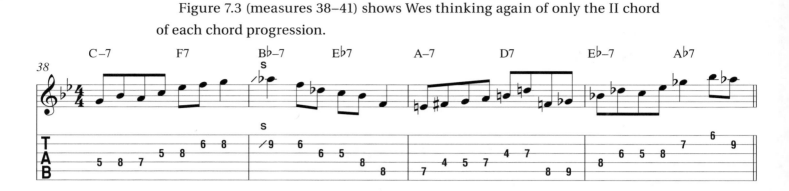

In figure 7.4 (measures 54–57), he slides chromatically into the 9 of the C–7 chord and then plays the 7 before playing the root and 7 of the F7 chord. Next, he plays an F–7 arpeggio over the Bb–7 chord, again disregarding the Eb7 chord. This generates the 5, 7, 9, and 11 of the Bb–7 chord. Over the A–7 chord, he plays a descending G major triad followed by the root and 7 of the D7 chord. He does not play over the last II V, but instead anticipates the G–7 chord that follows.

FIG. 7.4. "Four on Six" Measures 54–57

Figure 7.5 (measures 70 –73) is my personal favorite. Wes uses the b5 of the dominant chord in each measure to create tension, which makes for a very harmonically rich phrase.

In measure 70, he plays the 3 and 5 of C minor followed by the b5 of F7. He then sequences this idea a whole step down and plays the same idea over the Bb–7 to Eb7. In the next measure, he plays the 5 of the A–7 chord followed by the b5 of D7. Notice how he anticipates the D7 chord. The b5 is played on the upbeat of beat 1, and the D7 chord does not occur until beat 3.

FIG. 7.5. "Four on Six" Measures 70–73

FOUR ON SIX
Solo by Wes Montgomery

By John L. (Wes) Montgomery

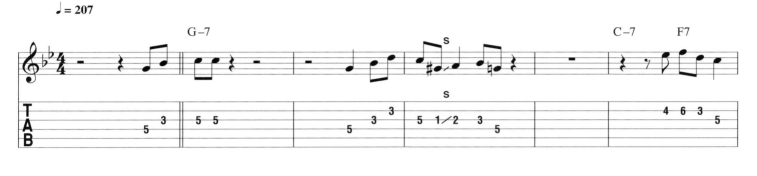

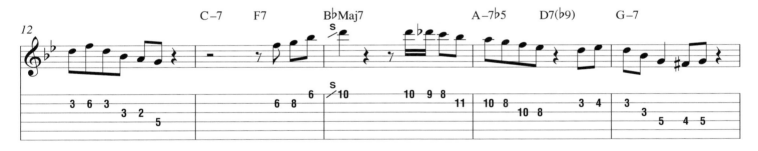

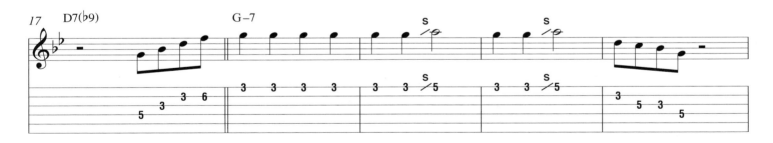

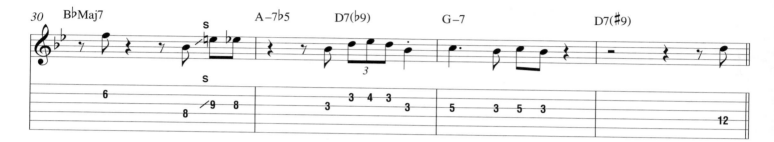

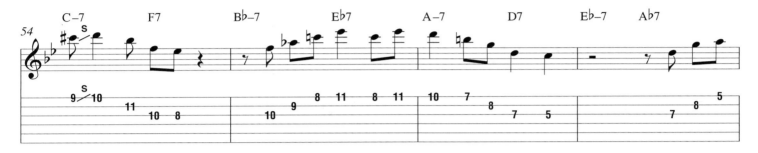

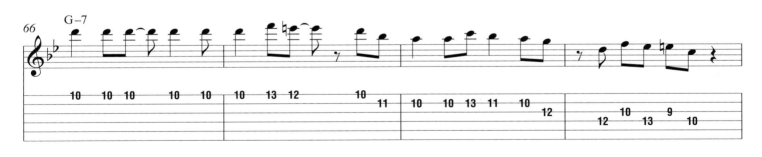

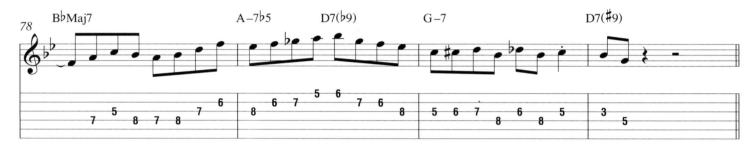

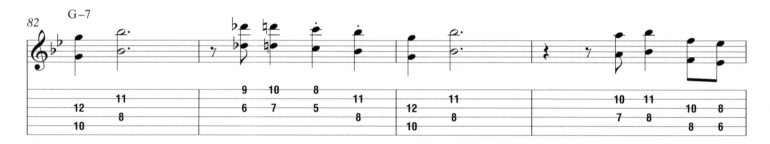

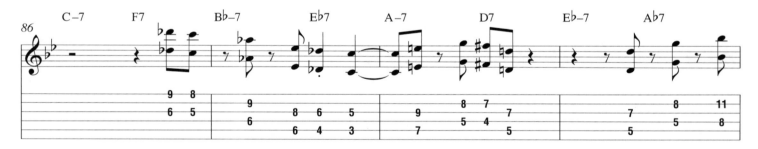

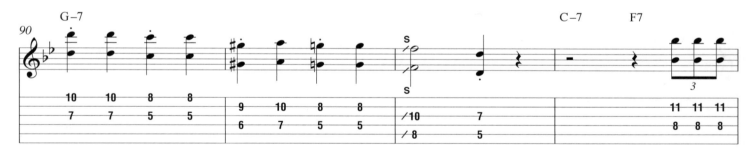

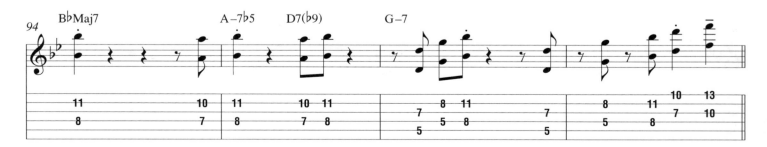

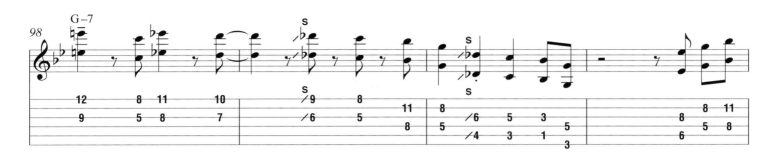

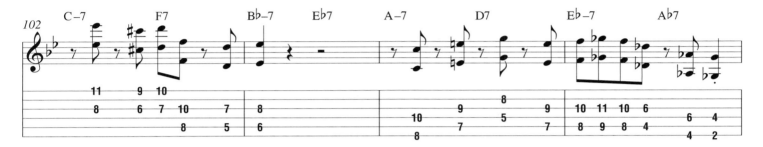

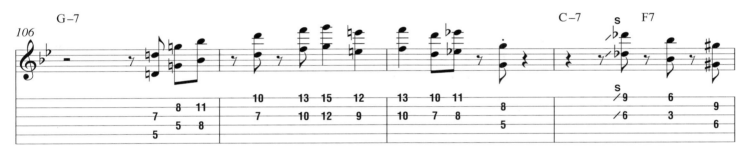

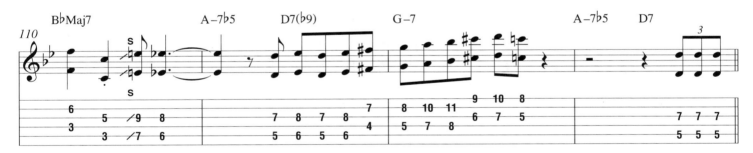

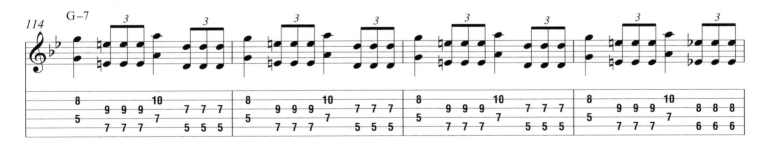

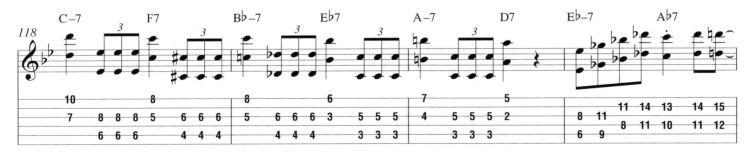

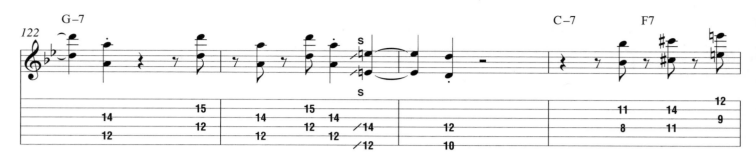

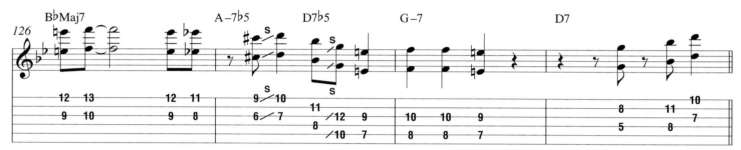

FIG. 7.6. "Four on Six" Complete Solo

8. WES MONTGOMERY

"Au Privave"

"Au Privave" was recorded on Cannonball Adderley's album *Cannonball Adderley and the Poll-Winners*. It was released in 1961 on the Riverside label and features Adderley on alto saxophone, Wes on guitar, Victor Feldman on piano and vibes, Ray Brown on bass, and Louis Hayes on drums. Wes frequently used basic arpeggio shapes to play major over minor, and we will explore this in figures 8.1 and 8.2. In figures 8.3 and 8.4, we will look at his use of the blues scale and sequencing.

Figure 8.1 shows Wes playing an E♭ major 7 arpeggio starting from the 7 over all four bars. By playing the E♭Maj7 arpeggio (relative to C minor), you get all of the "color tones" of the F7 (such as the 9, 11, and 13). This is one of the distinctive aspects of Wes's playing.

FIG. 8.1. "Au Privave" Measures 24–27

In figure 8.2, he plays a descending B major arpeggio over the A–7 to the D7 chord. He is probably thinking only of D7, or more importantly, the tritone substitution, which is the A♭. The relative major to A♭ is C♭ (or B), hence Wes's use of this arpeggio. It generated the ♯5, 3, ♭9, 13, and ♭5 of the D7 chord.

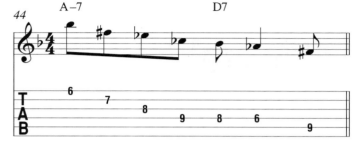

FIG. 8.2. "Au Privave" Measure 44

Figure 8.3 is a good example of Wes's use of the blues.

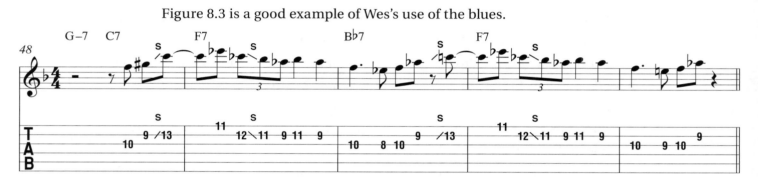

FIG. 8.3. "Au Privave" Measures 48–52

Figure 8.4 shows him sequencing the same idea: first, down a minor third, then down a fourth, and then down a fifth.

FIG. 8.4. "Au Privave" Measures 53–55

AU PRIVAVE
(Take One)
Solo by Wes Montgomery

By Charlie Parker

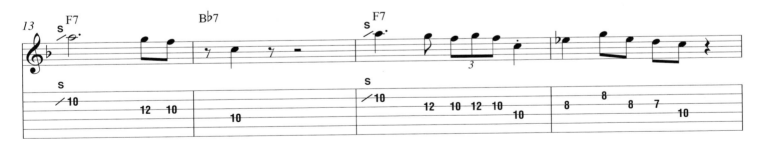

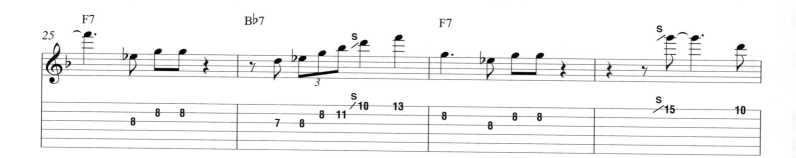

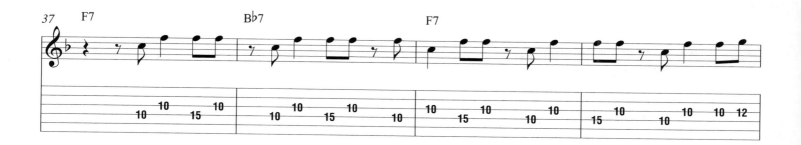

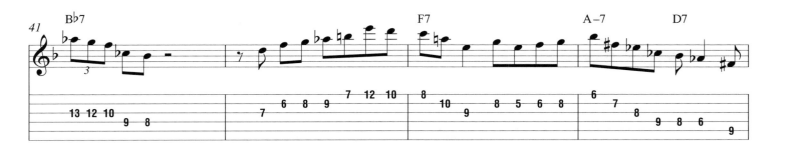

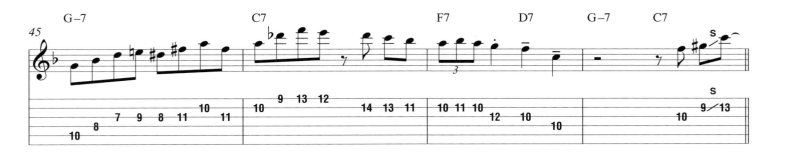

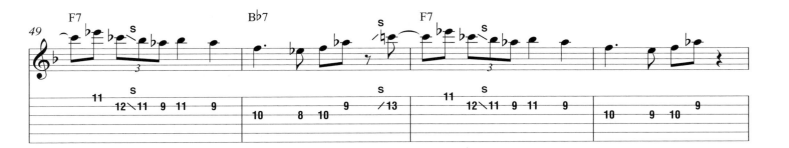

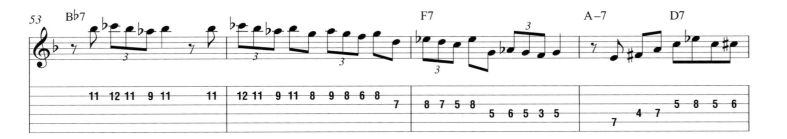

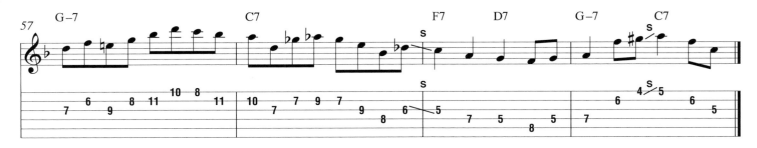

FIG. 8.5. "Au Privave" Complete Solo

"Yardbird Suite"

"Yardbird Suite" was recorded on Tal Farlow's 1957 album *The Swinging Guitar of Tal Farlow*. It features Eddie Costa on piano and Vinnie Burke on bass. The way that Tal plays this tune is very interesting. First, he plays the head in the original key of C, but the solos are in F. Second, the chords during the A sections of the solos change to all dominant chords descending by half step. We will look at four examples of how Tal plays these sections.

Figure 9.1 (measures 3–6) starts with an F major pentatonic phrase, with the exception of the B natural, which harmonically makes the chord an F7(♯11). On the E7, he lands on the ♯5 and then plays the 3, root, and 7 of the chord. Over the E♭7 chord, he starts on the 13 in addition to playing the major 7, 5, and ♯11. In the last measure, he encloses the root of the D7 chord by playing the ♭9 a half step above it, and a major 7 a half step below it. He finally plays the D and then proceeds to play the ♯5, root, natural 5, and the 11 of the D7.

FIG. 9.1. "Yardbird Suite" Measures 3–6

Figure 9.2 (measures 27–30) shows the exact same phrase as figure 9.1 over the E7 chord as well as the first three notes of the E♭7 chord being the same. This time, he rests over the D7 chord.

FIG. 9.2. "Yardbird Suite" Measures 27–30

Figure 9.3 (measures 35–38) has Tal starting with a descending F Mixolydian scale from the 3. As in figure 9.1, he uses a B-natural instead of a B-flat to make it an F7(♯11) chord.

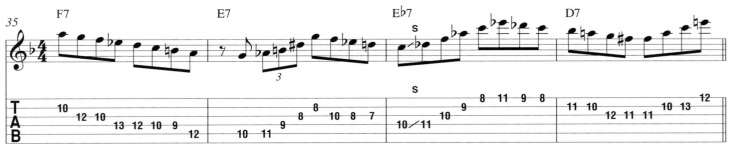

FIG. 9.3. "Yardbird Suite" Measures 35–38

Figure 9.4 (measures 91–94) combines many aspects of the three previous phrases. For example, the first measure is similar to figures 9.1 and 9.2. He still plays the major 3 of the E7 chord in measure 2. Over the E♭7 chord in the third measure, he plays the same phrase as figure 9.3, with the exception of the first and last notes. The D7 chord in the last measure is similar to figure 9.3.

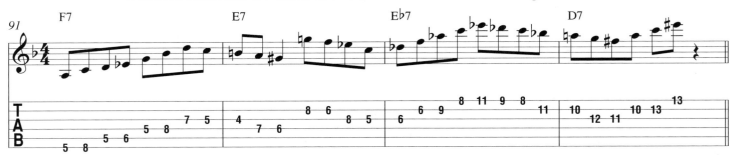

FIG. 9.4. "Yardbird Suite" Measures 91–94

YARDBIRD SUITE
Solo by Tal Farlow

By Charlie Parker

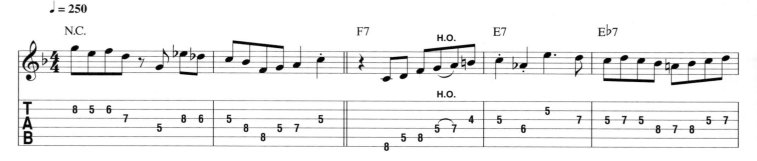

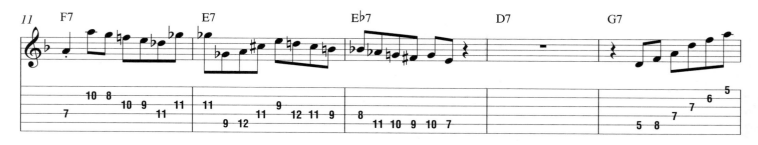

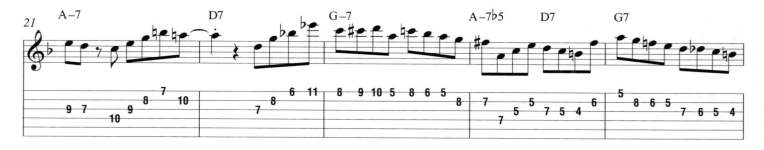

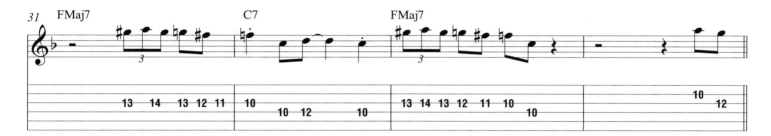

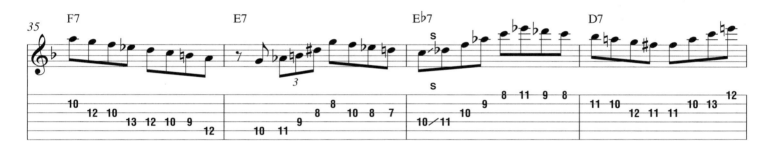

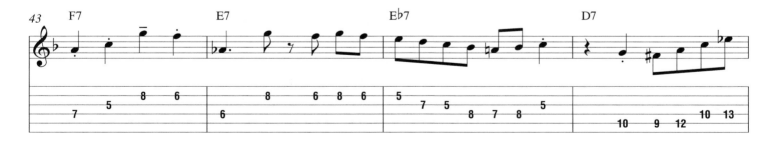

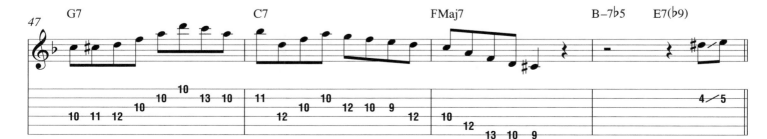

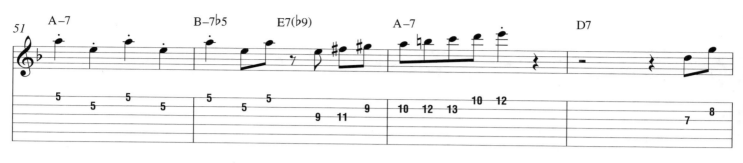

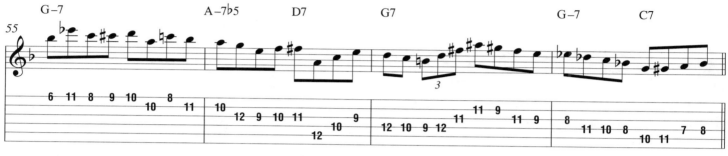

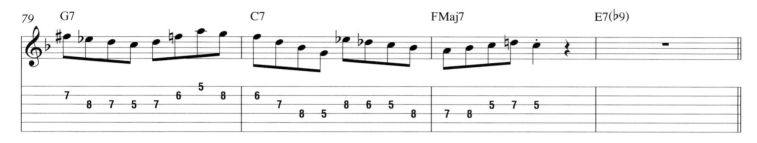

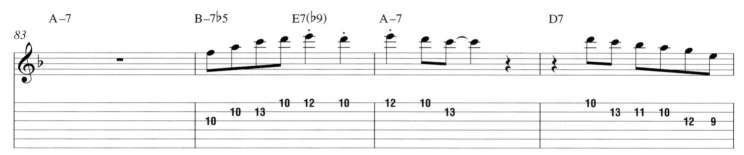

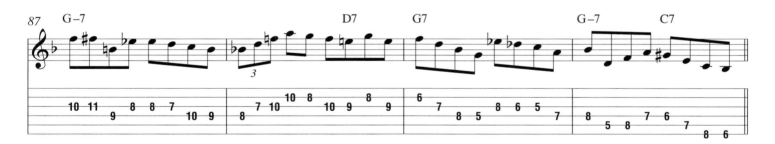

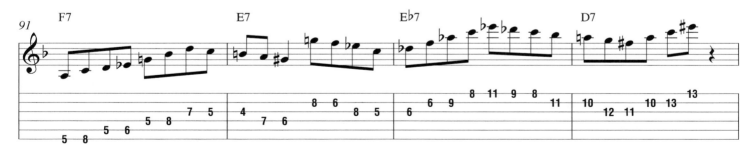

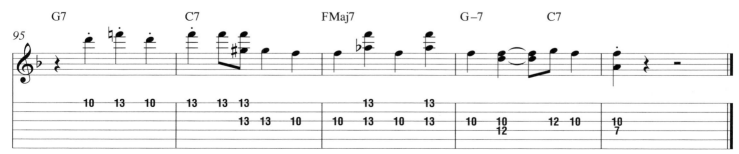

FIG. 9.5. "Yardbird Suite" Complete Solo

"All the Things You Are"

"All the Things You Are" was recorded on the album *This Is Tal Farlow* in 1958.

In this transcription, we will look at how Tal plays the VI II V I IV chord progression in the A sections. Notice how all of the phrases are different with the exception of the first three notes in figures 10.1 and 2. I suggest picking a few of these phrases that you like and transposing them to all keys, as the VI II V I IV chord progression is very common in jazz.

FIG. 10.1. "All the Things You Are" Measures 3–7

Figure 10.2 (measures 27–31) starts with the same 3 notes as figure 10.1.

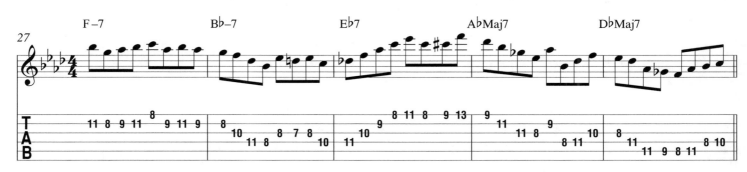

FIG. 10.2. "All the Things You Are" Measures 27–31

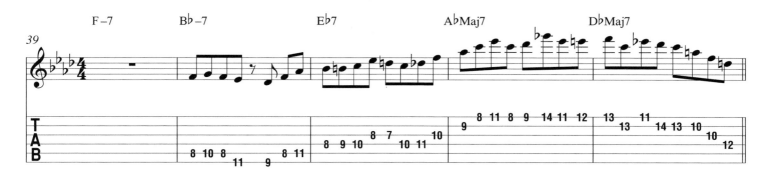

FIG. 10.3. "All the Things You Are" Measures 39–43

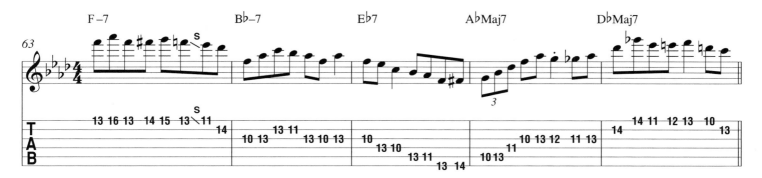

FIG. 10.4. "All the Things You Are" Measures 63–67

ALL THE THINGS YOU ARE
Solo by Tal Farlow

Lyrics by Oscar Hammerstein II
Music by Jerome Kern

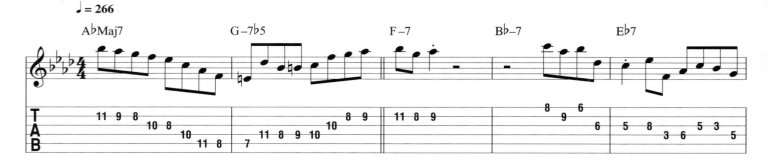

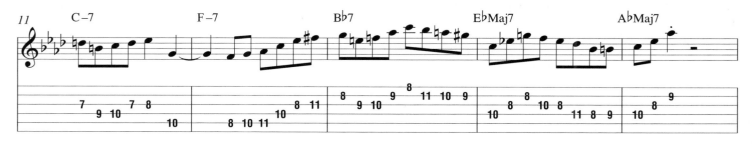

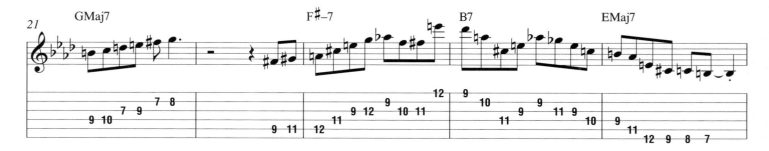

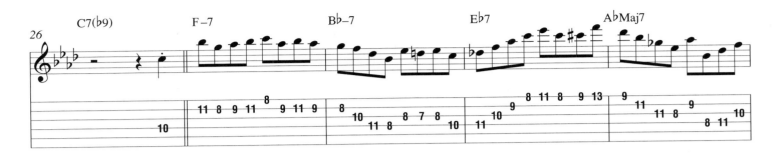

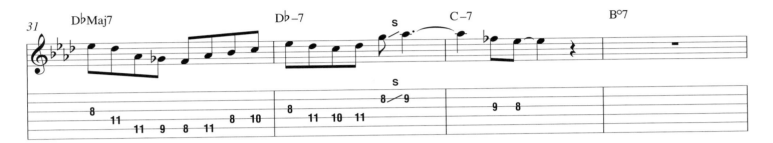

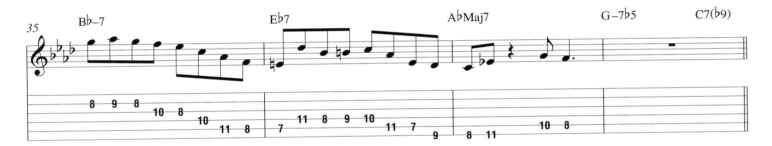

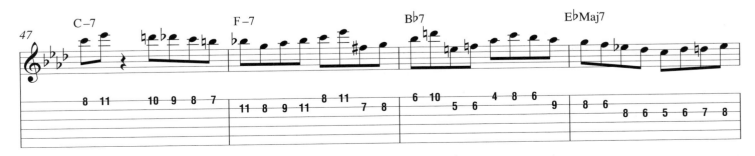

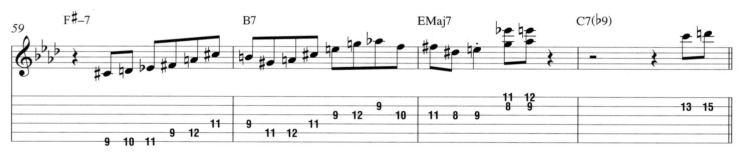

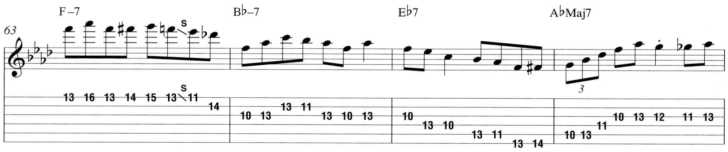

FIG. 10.5. "All the Things You Are" Complete Solo

11. GEORGE BENSON

"Stella by Starlight"

"Stella by Starlight" comes from George Benson's *Tenderly* album. It features a few different drummers on different tracks on the album as well as Ron Carter on bass and McCoy Tyner on piano. This song is played in the key of G instead of the usual B♭.

Figure 11.1 is a beautiful II V I phrase in C major. He uses the ♯5, ♯9, and ♭9 to create tension over the G7 chord before resolving to the 3 of C major.

FIG. 11.1. "Stella by Starlight" Measures 6–9

Figure 11.2 (measures 19–21) shows his use of the E altered dominant scale, also called the super Locrian scale, which is the seventh mode of F melodic minor. It is obvious that George is thinking F minor by his use of both the F minor triad and the A♭Maj7 arpeggio (relative to F minor).

FIG. 11.2. "Stella by Starlight" Measures 19–21

Figure 11.3 (measures 88–91) combines basic arpeggio shapes with a flurry of incredibly articulated, eighth note triplet figures. There is an ascending E♭ major 7 over the F7(♭9) chord. On the GMaj7 chord, he uses an ascending A–7♭5 arpeggio and a descending C–7. Although he uses basic arpeggios, it is what chords they are played over that makes the phrase, as well as that they are all played as eighth-note triplets, which makes for a very harmonically and rhythmically rich phrase.

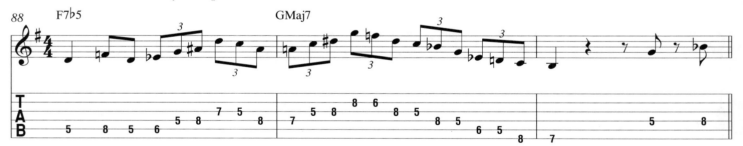

FIG. 11.3. "Stella by Starlight" Measures 88–91

STELLA BY STARLIGHT
Solo by George Benson

Words by Ned Washington
Music by Victor Young

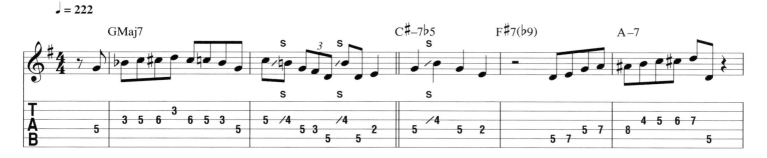

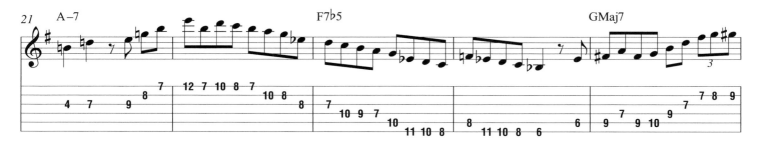

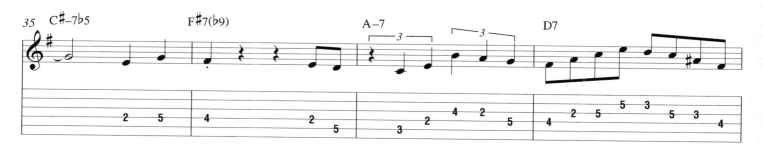

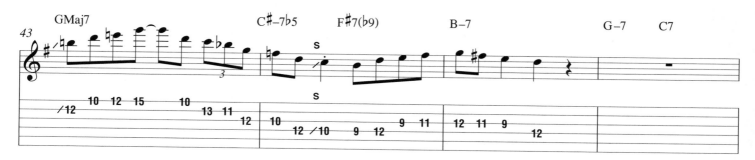

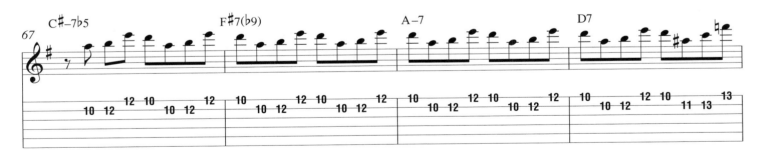

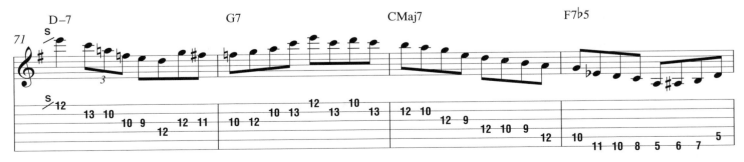

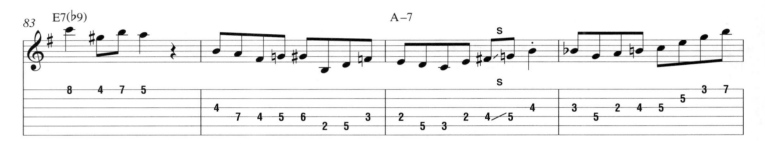

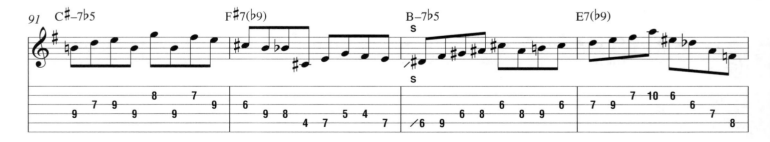

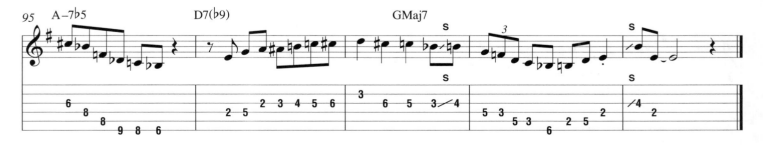

FIG. 11.4. "Stella by Starlight" Complete Solo

12. GEORGE BENSON

"I Could Write a Book"

"I Could Write a Book" also comes from George's *Tenderly* album. We are going to look at how George improvises over the ever so popular I VI II V chord progression.

Figure 12.1 (measures 3–7) is almost completely diatonic until the D7(♭9) chord where he plays the 3, 5, 7, and ♭9 of the chord. This is followed by a descending C♯–7 arpeggio over the C7 chord, which resolves to the 5 of the F major.

FIG. 12.1. "I Could Write a Book" Measures 3–7

Figure 12.2 (measures 19–22) is almost completely diatonic as well. However, he plays the ♭9 over the first D7 chord in measure 19.

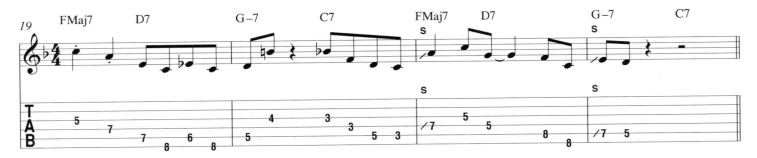

FIG. 12.2. "I Could Write a Book" Measures 19–22

Figure 12.3 (measures 51–54) is a great phrase in which he ends with a Bb major 7 arpeggio over the G minor 7 chord starting from the 7 (9, 3, 5, 7, and 9 of G minor), followed by the 13, #5, natural 5, and b5 of C7. Make sure to check out the second measure of this phrase.

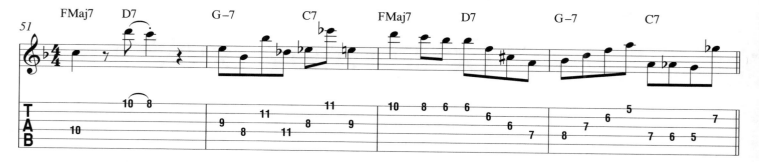

FIG. 12.3. "I Could Write a Book" Measures 51–54

In figure 12.4 (measures 63–66), George uses primarily descending D–7 and G–7 arpeggio shapes.

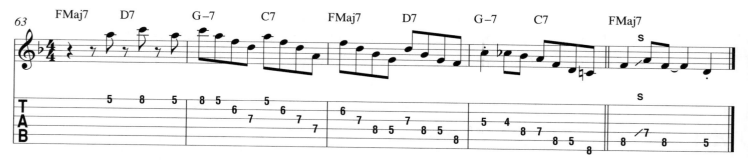

FIG. 12.4. "I Could Write a Book" Measures 63–67

I COULD WRITE A BOOK
Solo by George Benson

Words by Lorenz Hart
Music by Richard Rodgers

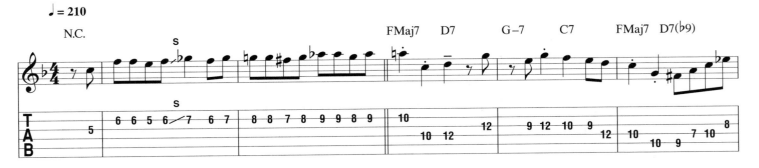

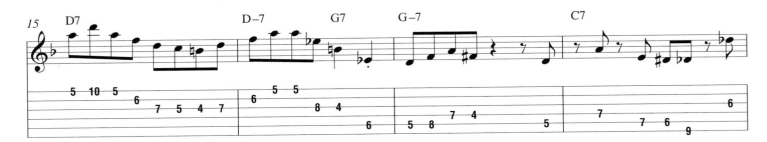

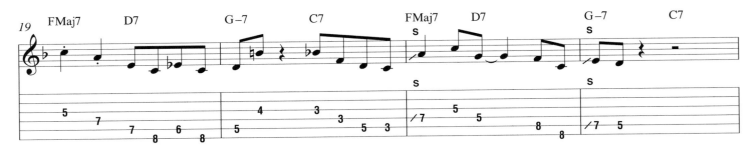

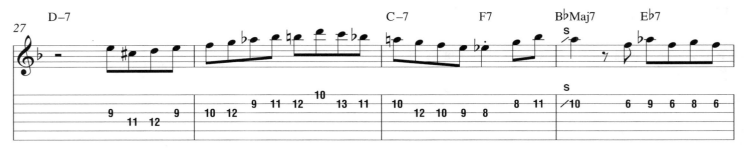

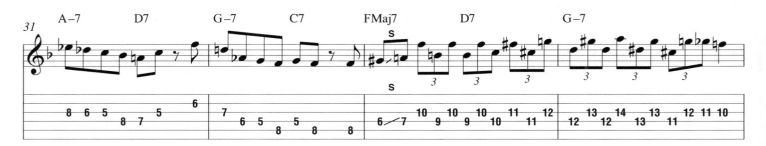

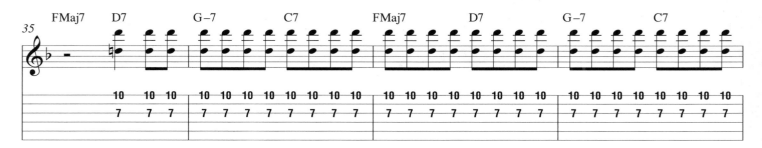

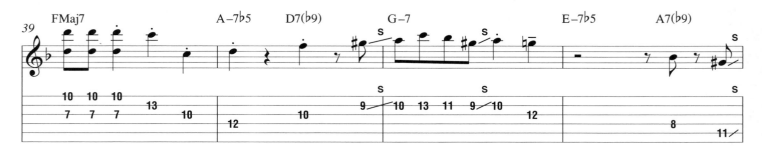

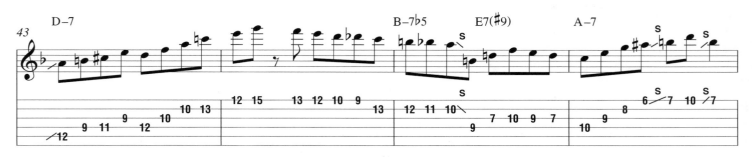

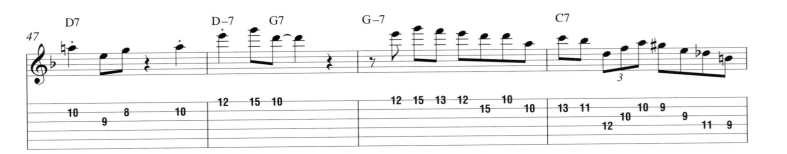

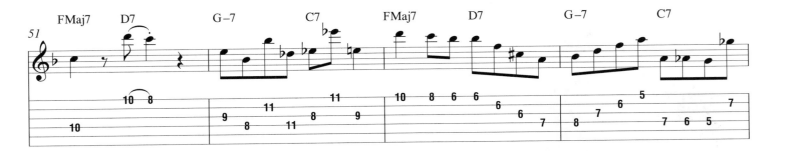

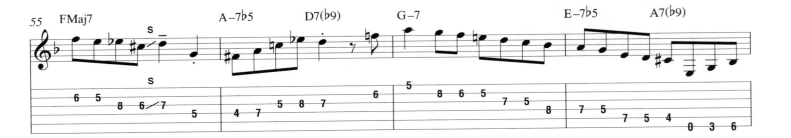

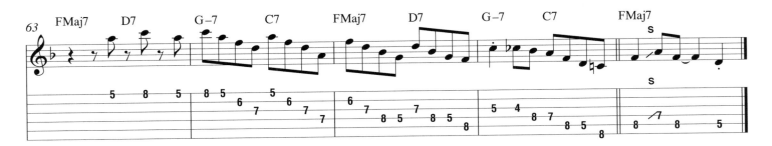

FIG. 12.5. "I Could Write a Book" Complete Solo

ABOUT THE AUTHOR

Photo by 和田安弘 *(Yasuhiro Wada)*

Michael Kaplan is a versatile guitarist with a bachelor's degree in classical guitar and a master's degree in jazz. He has performed, taught, and recorded in almost every musical style. While attending the University of Miami, Mr. Kaplan had the opportunity to study with internationally acclaimed guitarist Juan Mercadal, who also trained world-renowned guitarists Steve Morse and Manuel Barrueco. Some of Michael's performing credits include playing with Dr. Lonnie Smith, Alfred "Pee Wee" Ellis, Rich Little, and sharing the stage with the Average White Band. He also had the honor of playing under the baton of Michael Kamen.

Mr. Kaplan has given guitar lessons and workshops in all styles. He was on the faculty of Nova Southeastern University, Florida Atlantic University, Barry University, Miami Dade College, and Broward College. In addition, he was artist in residence at the Kathmandu Jazz Conservatory in Kathmandu, Nepal, where he was head of the guitar and bass department. Mr. Kaplan has taught courses in jazz and pop history, music theory, chamber music, and improvisation, as well as conducted jazz guitar ensembles, classical guitar ensembles, and jazz combos.

In addition, he has transcribed and edited a play-along book on jazz guitar comping with Jamey Aebersold and Dr. Mike Di Liddo. Currently, he is the director of the American Guitar Academy in Tokyo.